For Dan an

Thanks for being such amazing
                    us through all the craziness!!

You guys rock!

50dadjokes.com

Get ready to ignite laughter and tickle the funny bones of teachers with "50 Dad Jokes For Teachers." This rib-tickling assortment of puns, playful wordplay, and hilarious one-liners is specifically crafted to bring joy and amusement to our beloved educators.

From classroom antics to witty school scenarios, these jokes are bound to have teachers bursting with laughter in the staff room. With a touch of educational humor and a dash of silliness, this collection is perfect for any teacher seeking a delightful break from the daily grind.

So, buckle up and prepare for a side-splitting journey through the world of teacher-friendly humor. From math mishaps to science shenanigans, these unique jokes will leave teachers chuckling and remind them that laughter is indeed the best medicine. Get ready to share the gift of laughter with your favorite teachers and see why this collection is a must-have addition to their joke repertoire.

Why did the teacher wear sunglasses to school?

Because his students were too bright!

How do you organize a space-themed classroom?

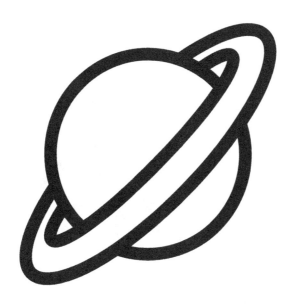

You planet!

What do you call a teacher who can rap?

The Notorious T.E.A.C.H!

Why did the teacher bring a ladder to the art room?

To reach the highest levels of creativity!

What do you call a teacher who never smiles?

A ruler!

What did the math book say to the unruly student?

"Let's work on these problems!"

What did the student say to the biology teacher?

"I find this class ribbiting!"

Why did the teacher bring a broom to the math class?

To sweep the problems under the rug!

Why did the teacher wear a crown in the classroom?

Because she ruled the school!

What do you call a teacher who crossed the busy highway?

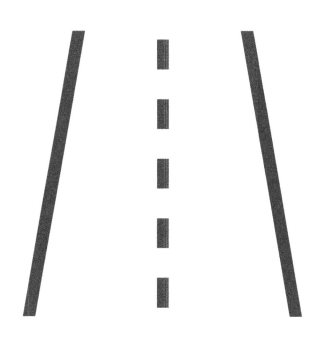

A brave educator on a field trip!

Why did the teacher wear a cape during the spelling test?

To be a super-visor!

Why was the computer teacher cold in class?

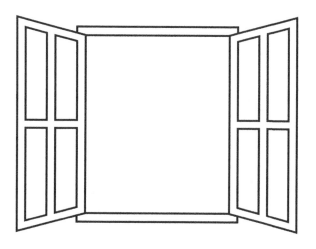

She left all the windows open!

What do you call a teacher who loves to tell jokes?

A pun-dit!

Why was the music teacher locked out of her classroom?

Because she lost the "keys"

How did the geography teacher teach map skills?

With a compass-ionate approach!

What's a teacher's favorite type of music?

"Class"-ick rock!

What did the teacher say to the student who didn't bring their pencil?

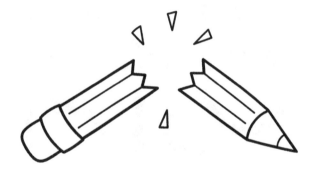

"You're really pointless today!"

Why did the teacher always carry a suitcase?

Because she wanted to make every lesson a trip!

What did the teacher say to the pencil sharpener?

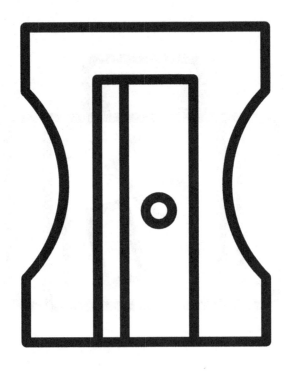

"That's an excellent point!"

How does a teacher stay cool in the summer?

With a fan club of students keeping them cool!

What's a teacher's favorite type of yoga?

"Class"-ana!

Why did the math teacher always have a calculator in the kitchen?

To help with the cook-culus!

What's a teacher's favorite exercise?

Grading papers – it's a real workout for the red pen!

Why did the teacher take the class to the bakery?

To prove that education is the best thing since sliced bread!

What do you call a teacher who never passes out assignments?

A myth-take!

What's a teacher's favorite dessert?

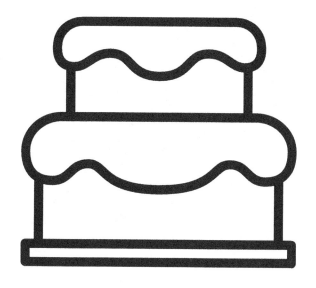

Anything "edu-cake-tional"!

Why did the teacher bring a flashlight to school?

To brighten the students' futures!

How did the geography teacher describe the Grand Canyon?

She said it was "quite the gap-tivating experience!"

What do you call a teacher who loves math?

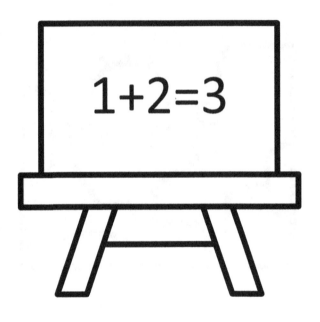

An "arithme-addict"!

Why did the teacher bring a hammer to the classroom?

Because they wanted to nail every lesson!

Why did the teacher wear a construction hat to the history lesson?

Because it was a lesson about "building" a better future!

What's a teacher's favorite insect?

The spelling bee!

Why did the teacher bring a suitcase full of markers to the classroom?

To "draw" attention to their lessons!

What's a teacher's favorite type of sandwich?

The "sub"-ject sandwich!

How did the teacher keep the classroom smelling fresh?

With some "common-scents"!

Why did the teacher always carry a bunch of keys?

Because they wanted to unlock knowledge!

What's a teacher's favorite type of coffee?

"Cram"-puccino!

What do you call a teacher who loves to garden?

A "seeds-ational" instructor!

What did the teacher say when the student complained about too much homework?

"Sorry, but it's 'home'-work, not 'vacation'-work!"

What's a teacher's favorite type of tree?

The knowledge tree – it's always branching out!

What did the teacher say to the student who kept interrupting the class?

"Please stop.
I'm trying to give you a
'lesson' in manners!"

What did the teacher say to the student who wanted to drop out of school?

"Don't pencil it in just yet – you have potential!"

What's a teacher's favorite type of plant?

A well-"rooted" student!

What do you call a teacher who loves to dance?

A "step"-teacher!

Why did the teacher bring a snorkel to the science class?

To dive deep into the subject matter!

What's a teacher's favorite type of fruit?

The "pear"-fectly educated student!

Why did the teacher bring a backpack full of rulers?

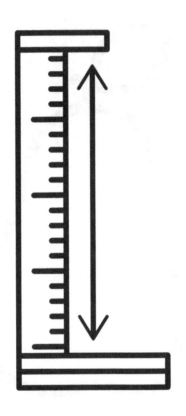

To measure their students' achievements!

What did the art teacher say to the student who didn't do their homework?

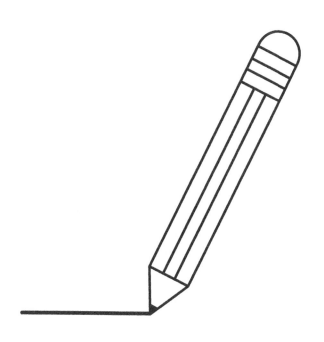

"You're really 'drawing' attention to yourself!"

Why did the teacher bring a binocular to the history class?

To help the students get a closer "look" at past events!

How did the teacher react when the student aced the test?

They said, "You're on a 'roll'-er coaster of success!"

Acknowledgements:

First, I want to thank my wife and son for supporting me in everything I do. You're love and support mean so much!

Secondly, thank you to my coworkers at Creed Interactive for helping me grow as a leader and for allowing me to practice some of these Dad Jokes on you! These books would never have happened without your encouragement and support!

Made in the USA
Las Vegas, NV
11 December 2023

82515939R00036